S0-AGC-595

WORLD BOOK'S
LIBRARY OF NATURAL DISASTERS
DROUGHTS

WORLD
BOOK

a Scott Fetzer company
Chicago
www.worldbookonline.com

World Book, Inc.
233 N. Michigan Avenue
Chicago, IL 60601
U.S.A.

For information about other World Book publications, visit our Web site at **http://www.worldbookonline.com** or call **1-800-WORLDBK (967-5325).**

For information about sales to schools and libraries, call **1-800-975-3250 (United States);** **1-800-837-5365 (Canada).**

2nd edition

The Library of Congress has cataloged an earlier edition of this title as follows:

Droughts.
     p. cm. -- (World Book's library of natural disasters)
    Summary: "A discussion of a major type of natural disaster, including descriptions of some of the most destructive; explanations of these phenomena, what causes them, and where they occur; and information about how to prepare for and survive these forces of nature. Features include an activity, glossary, list of resources, and index"--Provided by publisher.
    Includes bibliographical references and index.
    ISBN 978-0-7166-9803-6
    1. Droughts--Juvenile literature.
I. World Book, Inc.
QC929.25.D76 2007
363.34'929--dc22
                    2007008817

This edition:
ISBN: 978-0-7166-9819-7 (Droughts)
ISBN: 978-0-7166-9817-3 (set)

Printed in China
1 2 3 4 5 12 11 10 09 08

Editor in Chief: Paul A. Kobasa

Supplementary Publications

    Associate Director: Scott Thomas
    Managing Editor: Barbara A. Mayes

Editors: Jeff De La Rosa, Nicholas Kilzer, Christine Sullivan, Kristina A. Vaicikonis

Researchers: Cheryl Graham, Jacqueline Jasek

Manager, Contracts & Compliance (Rights & Permissions): Loranne K. Shields

Graphics and Design

    Associate Director: Sandra M. Dyrlund
    Associate Manager, Design: Brenda B. Tropinski
    Associate Manager, Photography: Tom Evans
    Designer: Matt Carrington

Production

    Director, Manufacturing and Pre-Press: Carma Fazio
    Manager, Manufacturing: Steven Hueppchen
    Manager, Production/Technology: Anne Fritzinger
    Proofreader: Emilie Schrage

Product development: Arcturus Publishing Limited

    Writer: Philip Steele
    Editors: Nicola Barber, Alex Woolf
    Designer: Jane Hawkins
    Illustrator: Stefan Chabluk

Acknowledgments:

AP Photo: 12 (Franck Prevel), 16 (Jamie Alexander), 23 (Jonathan Head).

Corbis: 4 (Vernon Bryant/ Dallas Morning News), 6 (Mary Ann Owen/ ZUMA), 7 (Blaine Harrington III), 10 (Nathan Benn), 13 (Penny Tweedie), 17, 29, 33, 43 (Reuters), 19 (Corbis), 22 (Amit Dave/ Reuters), 24 (Tom Bean), 26 (Galen Rowell), 27 (Niall Benvie), 28 (Will & Deni McIntyre), 30 (Chico Batata/ Diario do Amazonas/ epa), 31 (Rickey Rogers/ Reuters), 35 (Bruno Fert), 36 (Weda/ epa), 39 (Les Stone/ Sygma), 40 (David Gray/ Reuters), 41 (Stringer/ Australia/ Reuters), 42 (Bob Rowan/ Progressive Image).

Getty Images: 8 (William West/ AFP), 15 (Wesley/ Keystone), 37 (Issouf Sanogo/ AFP), 38 (Chris Jackson).

Science Photo Library: 20 (Scott Bauer/ US Department of Agriculture), 25 (Scharmer et al/ Royal Swedish Academy of Sciences).

Shutterstock: cover/ title page (Ximagination), 9 (Steve Simzer).

TABLE OF CONTENTS

Glossary There is a glossary of terms on pages 45-46. Terms defined in the glossary are in type **that looks like this** on their first appearance on any spread (two facing pages).

Additional resources Books for further reading and recommended Web sites are listed on page 47. Because of the nature of the Internet, some Web site addresses may have changed since publication. The publisher has no responsibility for any such changes or for the content of cited sources.

WHAT IS A DROUGHT?

A bridge, which once spanned water, crosses the dried bed of Lake Lavon, northeast of Dallas, Texas, in 2006, afters years of drought dramatically shrank the lake.

Regions of the world where people are at greatest risk of dying from the effects of drought.

A drought *(drowt)* is a condition that results when the average rainfall for an area drops far below the normal amount for a long time. Higher-than-normal temperatures usually go together with periods of drought. Because of this connection, we tend to think of droughts as hot, dry spells. The shortage of water has a great impact on plants, animals, and people.

Around the world

Drought depends on the usual rainfall in an area. A certain amount of rainfall might be normal in one region but too little in another. In the hot, dry **climate** of Libya, in North Africa, a drought

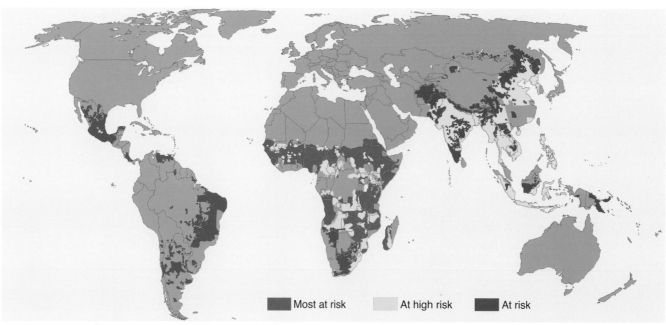

Most at risk　　At high risk　　At risk

Source: Natural Disaster Hotspots - A Global Risk Analysis © 2005 The World Bank and Columbia University.

could occur if less than 7 inches (180 millimeters) of rain fell in a year. But on the Indonesian island of Bali, which has a much wetter climate, a period of just six days without rain might be defined as a drought.

Average annual precipitation in different places

Precipitation is moisture that falls from clouds in any form, including rain, snow, or hail. Average precipitation varies around the world, and it can even differ greatly within continents.

DEFINING DROUGHT

Definitions of drought have varied around the world and over time. In 1887, a British scientist defined "absolute drought" in the United Kingdom as "15 consecutive days with less than 0.01 inch (0.3 centimeter) of rain on any one day." This definition was abandoned 100 years later. In 1937, the U.S. Weather Bureau (now called the National Weather Service) defined drought as "a period when rainfall is 30 percent of average for 21 days or longer." Today, meteorologists use more relative descriptions to define drought. **Meteorological** *(mee tee uh rah LAHJ ih kuhl)* **drought** occurs when there is less precipitation than usual in a particular area at a particular time. A region experiences **hydrological** *(hy drah LAHJ ih kuhl)* **drought** when the levels of its surface water, such as lakes and streams, and its underground water fall below normal levels. An **agricultural drought** occurs when conditions in an area—such as precipitation and water level—fall below what the crops in the area need to grow.

Continent	Place	Highest and lowest average annual precipitation extremes in inches (in) [centimeters (cm)]
Africa	Debundscha, Cameroon	405 in (1,029 cm)
	Wadi Halfa, Sudan	less than 0.1 in (less than 0.3 cm)
Asia	Mawsynram, India	467.4 in (1,187 cm)
	Aden, Yemen	1.8 in (4.6 cm)
Australia	Bellenden Ker, Queensland	340 in (863.6 cm)
	Mulka, South Australia	4.05 in (10.3 cm)
Europe	Crkvica, Bosnia-Herzegovina	183 in (464.8 cm)
	Astrakhan, Russia	6.4 in (16.3 cm)
North America	Henderson Lake, British Columbia	256 in (650.2 cm)
	Batagues, Mexico	1.2 in (3 cm)
South America	Quibdo, Colombia	354 in (899.2 cm)
	Arica, Chile	0.03 in (0.08 cm)

Source: U.S. National Climatic Data Center.

THE IMPACTS OF DROUGHT

The impacts of drought

Drought can have a devastating effect on a region. But unlike nearly all other natural hazards, a drought develops over time. At first, a drought may not be as catastrophic as an earthquake or a **hurricane,** but some climate experts consider drought to be the most damaging of all natural disasters. According to the United Nations, droughts were responsible for over 280,000 deaths from 1991 to 2000 alone. Droughts have a disastrous effect on the **environment** because the world's most precious resource—water—becomes scarce.

Dwindling water sources

Over time, lack of rain causes rivers, streams, lakes, and ponds to carry less water and eventually to dry up. Drought also affects the **groundwater** that lies beneath Earth's surface. Groundwater comes mainly from rain and melted

The white water line on the rocks reveals a dramatic drop in 2004 in the water level of Lake Mead after several years of drought. The lake is a reservoir made by the Hoover Dam on the Colorado River, which receives most of its water from snowmelt in the Rocky Mountains.

snow. It supplies the water for wells and springs. If people keep using their usual amounts of water during a drought, the level of groundwater—called the **water table**—drops, often causing the land surface to crack and sink. This movement can damage buildings, roads, and pipelines. The lowering of the water table creates particular problems in coastal areas because salt water from the sea can seep into underground **reservoirs** *(REHZ uhr vwahrz)* and make the water undrinkable.

Chain reaction

Many of the world's rivers receive a large proportion of their water from mountainous regions. These regions act as the world's reservoirs, feeding streams and rivers with runoff rainwater and melted snow even during dry periods. However, if there is less rainfall or snow than usual in a mountain region, the **headwaters** of the rivers flowing out of this region will carry less water, affecting areas downstream. The situation becomes worse if people have built dams across the rivers to store or draw off water. Water shortages may develop even great distances from the original location of the drought.

EARLY CIVILIZATIONS

The world's first civilizations arose in river valleys. The earliest civilization developed about 5,500 years ago in the valleys of the Tigris and Euphrates rivers in the Middle East. Other civilizations developed beside the Nile River in Egypt, the Indus River in what are now Pakistan and northwestern India, the Huang He (Yellow River) in China, and the Andes Mountains of present-day Peru. All of these regions were affected by drought from time to time. Experts believe that the Old Kingdom of Egypt may have ended in 2150 B.C. because of a long-lasting drought.

The Salto Grande waterfall is fed by water that flows down from the high, snow-covered peaks of the Andes Mountains in Chile. Lower down, the river creates lakes, which expand or shrink based on the flow from above.

During a **hydrological drought,** an area's surface and underground supplies of water for agricultural, industrial, and personal uses are often reduced. Although drought has an impact on people in towns and cities, its effects are often most visible in the countryside, where land simply dries up. In some areas, dry, crumbly topsoil might be blown away by the wind, wearing away the land and leaving barren patches of earth.

Agricultural drought

When reduced rainfall or water supplies begin to affect farmers and their crops, **meteorologists** say that region is experiencing an **agricultural drought.** An agricultural drought occurs when the soil does not contain enough moisture to meet the needs of crops growing in the area. The impact depends on the kinds of crops that farmers are trying to raise and the stage of their growth. A dry period may cause an agricultural drought when young plants are growing. But farmers might consider dry weather to be helpful when cereal grains are ripening.

An Australian farmer near Wimmera, northwest of Melbourne, inspects wheat stunted by an extended drought.

A sprinkler keeps a lawn green during the summer months. During a drought, the use of sprinklers and the washing of cars are usually banned to conserve water.

Supply and demand

A severe drought quickly affects the delivery of goods and services, including water itself, to communities. To deal with water shortages, public officials often introduce water rationing throughout a region. At first, rationing may involve restrictions on such activities as watering lawns and washing cars. If the drought continues, a city's public water supply may be turned off at certain times of the day. However, water rationing may depend on demand. If people **conserve** water by cutting down on the amount they use, the impact of a drought may not be so severe.

CLIMATE CHANGE

Most scientists agree that Earth's climate is changing. The average temperature of Earth's surface is gradually increasing in a phenomenon known as **global warming.** Scientists believe that this warming effect may result in more droughts. **Meteorologists** at the U.S. National Center for Atmospheric Research reported in 2005 that the area of the world affected by serious drought has doubled in the last 30 years. In the 1970's, 10 to 15 percent of Earth was found to be "very dry." By the early 2000's, this figure had risen to nearly 30 percent.

DROUGHTS OF THE PAST

Historians believe that many disastrous droughts occurred in prehistoric and ancient times. However, since no one knows how many ancestors of modern human beings were alive in those days, it is difficult to estimate how devastating such droughts may have been.

Mysterious endings

Some of the world's great empires and cultures came to an end under circumstances that historians have long considered mysterious. Modern historians now think that disastrous droughts may have played their part in the downfall of these civilizations. For example, the powerful kingdom of Akkad in Mesopotamia ended when people began to move away from the region in huge numbers in about 2200 B.C. Archaeologists have found evidence that a severe drought that lasted for some 300 years turned the region's wheat fields into desert. Droughts also may have contributed to the end of the Moche *(MOH chay)* civilization of Peru in about A.D. 600, to the Classic Period of the Maya culture in Mexico and Central America in about 900; and to the Chaco Canyon culture of New Mexico in about 1150.

The ruins of a Moche pyramid in the dry, barren landscape of northern Peru. Archaeologists believe that drought may have contributed to the end of the Moche civilization in about A.D. 600.

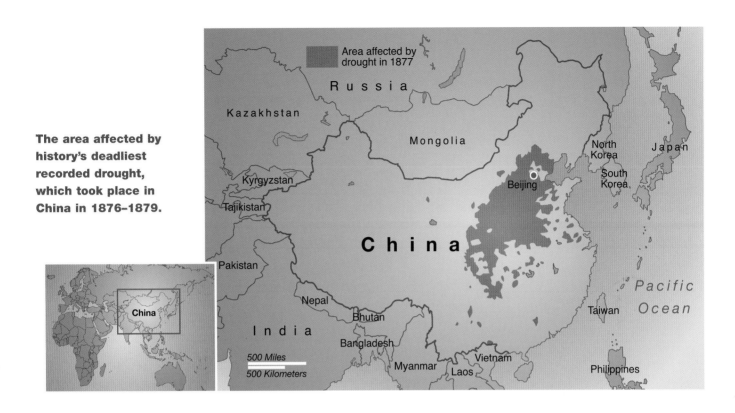

The area affected by history's deadliest recorded drought, which took place in China in 1876–1879.

China, late 1800's

The deadliest drought in recorded history occurred in China from 1876 to 1879. It is thought to have affected more than 100 million people and to have killed from 9 to 13 million people across many Chinese provinces. As many as 5 million people starved in the northern province of Shaanxi, where virtually no rain fell throughout the three-year period. Some reports tell of children being sold by starving parents to families in parts of China not affected by the drought. Others describe poor farmers eating their houses to survive (the houses of poor farmers at the time were often built of corn stems and rice and wheat straw). Another 1 million Chinese starved to death in a drought that lasted from 1892 to 1894.

TREE EVIDENCE

Scientists can learn about past **climates** by studying the growth rings in trees that have been cut. Some kinds of trees make a new layer of wood each year. These layers form a series of rings. During years of drought, a tree does not grow as much as it does during a normal year, and its annual rings are correspondingly narrower. Tree rings have revealed that a drought, known as the Great Drought, struck the southwest region of North America between 1276 and 1299. During this time, many Native American groups left their villages in present-day New Mexico and Arizona in search of food and water. One of these groups, the Hopi, developed a special ceremony to ask spirits to send rain. The ceremony included a dance in which the participants put live rattlesnakes in their mouths.

HEAT WAVES

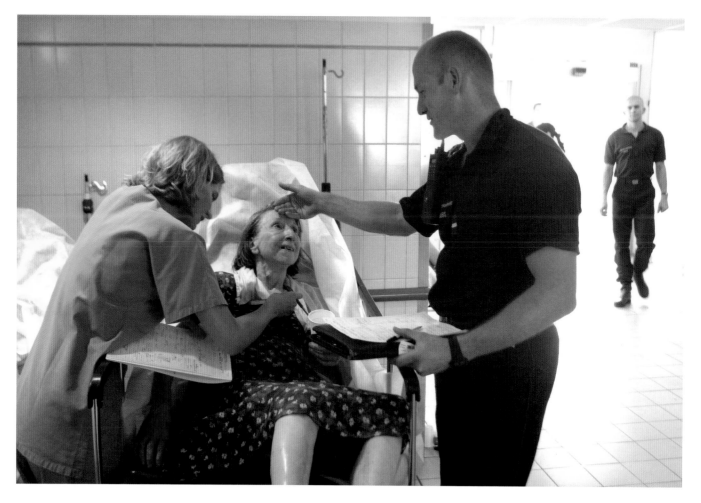

Medics look after an elderly woman at a Paris hospital during a heat wave in August 2003. Thousands of people, particularly the elderly, needed hospital treatment because of record high temperatures.

A **heat wave** is a period of very hot weather. The term is ordinarily used when a particular region has hotter-than-normal weather for at least several days. For example, a strong heat wave that began in France and other nearby countries in June 2003 and lasted until August caused the hottest summer in Europe for at least 500 years. Several countries posted record temperatures, including the United Kingdom, which reached a high of over 100 °F (38 °C) for the first time since record keeping began. More than 52,000 people died from heat-related causes throughout all of Europe, including nearly 15,000 in France and more than 18,000 in Italy.

High pressure

Heat waves, as well as many droughts, are caused by areas of high **atmospheric pressure,** sometimes called *highs.* Highs develop where air pushes downward. When air is compressed in this way, it warms up and the amount of moisture it holds falls. As a result, clouds do not form. Highs are massive **weather systems** that can become stalled over a region.

Ash Wednesday during a heat wave

In Australia, a drought that lasted from April 1982 into 1983 was accompanied by a heat wave in which the temperature rose to 109.4 °F (43 °C). The heat sparked some 180 **wildfires** on Ash Wednesday, Feb. 16, 1983, which killed 76 people and hundreds of thousands of sheep and other livestock.

Cattle and other livestock suffer from a lack of water and grass for grazing during heat waves and droughts, such as this 1983 drought in New South Wales, Australia.

HEAT INDEX

Heat waves can be very dangerous, especially for young children and the elderly, whose bodies are not strong enough to withstand high temperatures. Lengthy exposure to high temperatures can result in *heat cramps* (muscle cramps caused by loss of salt and water), *heat exhaustion* (characterized by cold, clammy skin and the general symptoms of shock), and *heatstroke* (a potentially life-threatening condition).

The U.S. National Weather Service uses a heat index to warn people of the dangers of very hot weather. The index is a measure of how hot the air feels and describes possible heat disorders for people in high-risk groups.

80–90 °F (26.7–32.2 °C)	Fatigue possible with prolonged exposure or physical activity
90–105 °F (32.2–40.6 °C)	**Sunstroke,** heat cramps, or heat exhaustion possible with prolonged exposure or physical activity
105–130 °F (40.6–54.4 °C)	Sunstroke, heat cramps, or heat exhaustion likely, and heatstroke possible, with prolonged exposure or physical activity
130 °F (54.4 °C) or higher	Heatstroke or sunstroke highly likely with continued exposure

EUROPE 1975–1976

Large parts of Europe experienced a major drought that began in May 1975 and lasted until the end of summer 1976. The affected region stretched from northeastern Russia and Scandinavia in the north to Spain and Turkey in the south. The drought was especially severe in Sweden, the United Kingdom, the Netherlands, and Spain.

The European drought of 1975–1976 affected the whole of Europe and most of Turkey.

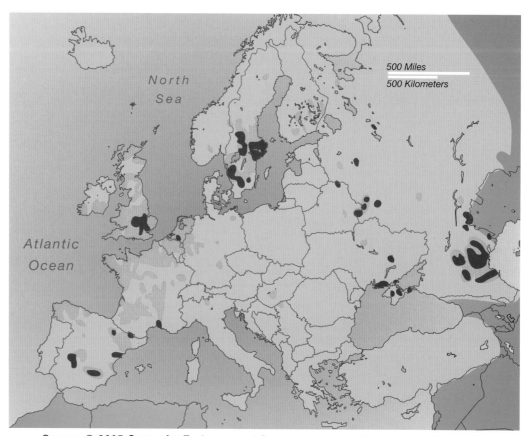

North Sea

Atlantic Ocean

500 Miles
500 Kilometers

Key:

- Severely affected by drought
- Badly affected by drought
- Affected by drought

Source: © 2005 Center for Environmental Systems Research, University of Kassel, Germany.

Blocking high

Sometimes the weather seems to get stuck and remain the same for weeks or even months. **Meteorologists** call this weather pattern *blocking*. Such a pattern formed over the United Kingdom in 1976, when a blocking high settled over the whole country during June and July. Temperatures topped 90 °F (32 °C) for 14 days in a row in southern England. Television weather reports showed **satellite** photographs of the United Kingdom without a single cloud over the country. In southwest England, no rain fell at all for 45 days in a row, an unusual condition for a country known for its changeable and usually mild weather.

Fires and water shortages

In 1976, less than half the normal amount of rain fell in many parts of Europe. By summer, many **reservoirs** were almost empty. Grass and forest fires broke out in the United Kingdom, France, and Spain. In the United Kingdom, crops failed, and farmers suffered losses of more than $900 million. In towns and cities, the dried-out ground and dropping of the **water table** caused many houses to shift and sink.

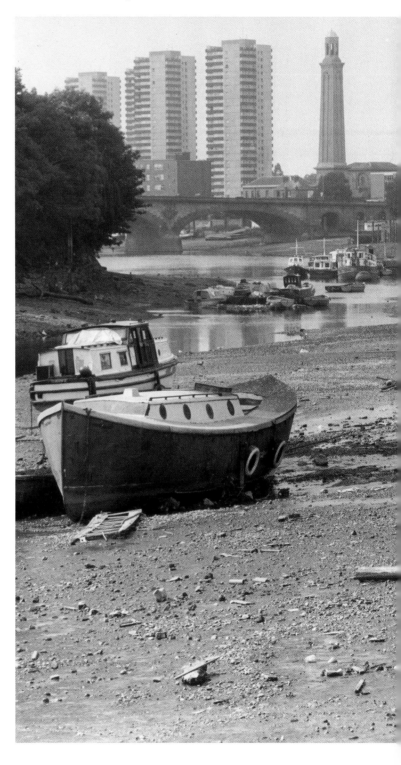

Boats lie stranded on the dried-up riverbed of the Thames near Kew, in the United Kingdom, during the drought of 1976.

DROUGHT MINISTER

In 1976, water restrictions were introduced in many parts of Europe, including the United Kingdom. First, the use of hoses to water outdoor plantings was banned, and then water supplies were cut off altogether in some areas. People had to get their water from pipes in the street or from water tankers. In August, the British government appointed a minister for drought, giving him special emergency powers. People who did not obey the new restrictions were taken to court and were heavily fined. The drought finally ended in October 1976.

WIND AND DUST

Land dries up during a drought, and topsoil loses its moisture. Such conditions can have devastating effects once winds start to blow. Soil particles stick together when they are wet, but when they dry out, the particles separate and can easily be blown away. The smaller the soil particles, the lower the wind speed that is needed to move them.

Dust storms

A dust storm occurs when strong winds pick up and carry fine particles of earth for long distances. Most of these particles measure less than $\frac{1}{400}$ inch (0.0625 millimeter). When they fall back to the ground, the wind continues to push them forward, and they knock other particles loose. As the dust storm builds, many particles stay suspended in the air. The storm may cover hundreds of miles and rise to a height of more than 10,000 feet (3,000 meters). In the United States, **meteorologists** announce a dust storm warning if dust makes it impossible to see past ¼ mile (400 meters) and winds reach 25 miles (40 kilometers) per hour.

A huge dust storm rolls over the Australian town of Griffith, 248 miles (400 kilometers) southwest of Sydney, on Nov. 29, 2002, after high winds whipped up dry top soil, the result of a period of prolonged drought.

California drought

Very low rainfall over many months in California in 1975 to 1977 led to such a severe shortage of water that 31 of the state's 58 counties were declared disaster areas. Toward the end of the drought, a terrible dust storm blew up in the San Joaquin Valley. The wind reached 192 miles (309 kilometers) per hour—the force of the highest-category **hurricane**—and lifted more than 25 million tons (22.8 million metric tons) of soil from the land. Soil and sand drifted, piled up, and buried roads and cars. A large area of the valley was changed from fertile farmland to barren, sandy soil.

CHINESE DUST

On several days in April 2001, people in Denver and other areas of Colorado noticed that they could not see the Rocky Mountains because a white, dusty haze blocked their view. They were amazed to learn from news bulletins that this dust cloud—which stretched for nearly 1,250 miles (2,000 kilometers)—had blown all the way from China. Winds often pick up soil from China's northwestern region during periods of drought. Such dust clouds travel east for hundreds of miles, where they pick up particles of industrial pollutants from Beijing and other cities and then cross the Pacific Ocean to North America. Meteorologists followed the progress of the dust cloud all the way across the United States to the East Coast, where it finally moved off over the Atlantic Ocean.

Pedestrians and cyclists shield their faces during a dust storm in the industrial city of Chengdu, in southern China. The dust storm actually turned the sky yellow as it struck the city.

DUST BOWL

A series of dust storms that struck the southern Great Plains of the United States in the 1930's became one of the worst environmental disasters in the country's history. A severe drought began in the area in 1931 and lasted until 1938. The soil—which was already over-grazed by livestock and deeply plowed to grow wheat—dried out. Crops failed and prairie grasses died off. As the natural vegetation and farm crops disappeared, the soil was left bare. Soon vast dust storms began to blow, stripping away tons of topsoil and devastating farms and rangeland.

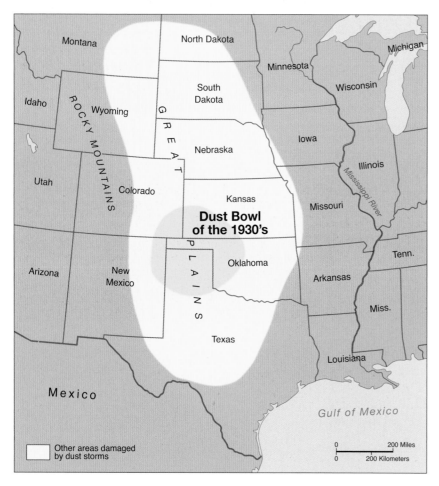

The Dust Bowl of the 1930's was centered in the Panhandle of Oklahoma and Texas and in southwest Kansas. This region suffered terrible dust storms again in the 1950's and 1970's.

Affected region

The drought region came to be known as the *Dust Bowl.* Altogether, dust storms damaged about 50 million acres (20 million hectares) of land, mainly in Colorado, Kansas, New Mexico, Oklahoma, and Texas. One of the first major storms struck in May 1934. It carried about 350 million tons (318 million metric tons) of dirt all the way to the East Coast. In 1937, more than 100 big storms swept through the Dust Bowl.

Black blizzards

The clouds of dust and sand were so thick that they blocked out the sun for days. People named the storms "black blizzards." The worst of these

storms occurred on April 14, 1935, a day that became known as Black Sunday. The storm was so intense that day was turned into night, and many people feared that the end of the world had arrived.

After a while, settlers claimed that they could tell what state dust was blowing from based on its color: dirt from Oklahoma was red and from New Mexico, gray. People and animals caught in a storm experienced severe lung damage from breathing the gritty dust. Cars and farm machines were ruined, as their engines clogged. Dirt had to be shoveled out of houses and plowed off roadways. The region's agricultural base collapsed, and by 1940, 2.5 million people had left the area in search of work elsewhere.

A huge 1930's dust storm blots out the sky as it approaches a farm in the Dust Bowl, an area of severe drought in the southern Great Plains.

THE GRAPES OF WRATH

The novel *The Grapes of Wrath,* by U.S. author John Steinbeck, was published in 1939. It tells the story of the Joad family of Oklahoma, whose farm fails during the 1930's drought. In the book, Steinbeck describes a dust storm: "The finest dust did not settle back to earth now, but disappeared into the darkening sky. The wind grew stronger, whisked under stones, carried up straws and old leaves, and even little clods. ... The air and the sky darkened and through them the sun shone redly, and there was a raw sting in the air. ... Men and women huddled in their houses, and they tied handkerchiefs over their noses when they went out, and wore goggles to protect their eyes."

MEASURING DROUGHT

Meteorologists measure and classify droughts in various ways. Their goal is to compare moisture conditions at different times or in different places so that they can learn more about droughts and predict when they might occur.

Kinds of drought

Besides **meteorological, agricultural,** and **hydrological** drought, weather experts also sometimes use other terms to describe drought:

A meteorologist checks a rain gauge in Colorado as part of a project researching the effect of drought on U.S. grasslands.

- *Permanent drought* occurs in the driest **climates,** such as deserts, where people can grow crops only on **irrigated** land.

- *Seasonal drought* occurs in places with annual rainy and dry seasons.

- *Unpredictable drought* can occur almost anywhere without warning, but it is usually found in less dry regions when normal rains fail.

- *Invisible drought* is a dry spell that may have occasional showers but not enough rain to refill a low **water table,** so that most moisture **evaporates.**

The Palmer Drought Severity Index

In 1965, U.S. meteorologist Wayne Palmer invented a way to measure and grade droughts. He developed a scale that runs from –4 for extreme drought to +4 for extremely wet conditions. A figure on the scale for any particular location is determined by measuring the amount of **precipitation,** the temperature, and the level of moisture in the soil. The Palmer index is useful for tracking long-term droughts over several months or even years.

Predicting the future

Scientists, farmers, and **environmentalists** have learned a great deal about drought from studying past events. Yet it is still difficult for **meteorologists** to forecast the weather very far into the future. Researchers continually strive to improve the technology forecasters use. In the United States, the National Drought Mitigation Center helps develop measures to reduce vulnerability to drought. Experts call this process *drought planning.* By 2006, more than three-fourths of the individual states had a plan for dealing with the next drought.

FORECASTING BY TRADITION

The Kamba people of eastern Kenya have their own traditional ways of predicting drought. Knowing when the area will be under a dry spell is important because many Kamba families rely on small farming plots for food. They watch plant and animal behavior closely. They start to store food and to move their cattle to relatives who live on more fertile land when any of the following begin to happen:

- The kivingo tree (which does not usually bud) starts to flower.
- The kinguthe plant flowers before any other plant.
- Crop-destroying insects start to appear.
- A cold, light mist (which the Kamba call miki) appears.
- The nights become very cold.
- Dry, cold, fierce winds sweep across the land.

A map produced weekly by the Climate Prediction Center of the United States based on the Palmer Drought Severity Index.

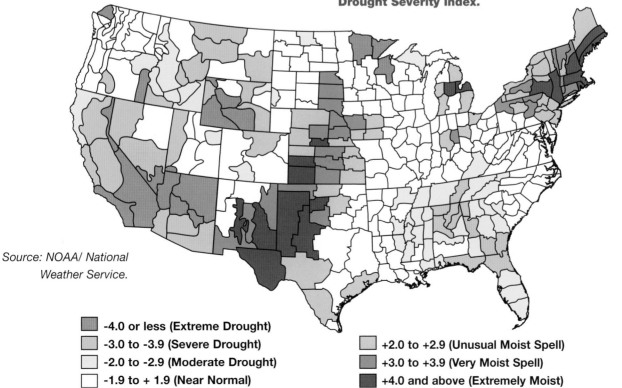

Source: NOAA/ National Weather Service.

- -4.0 or less (Extreme Drought)
- -3.0 to -3.9 (Severe Drought)
- -2.0 to -2.9 (Moderate Drought)
- -1.9 to + 1.9 (Near Normal)
- +2.0 to +2.9 (Unusual Moist Spell)
- +3.0 to +3.9 (Very Moist Spell)
- +4.0 and above (Extremely Moist)

SEASONS AND CYCLES

Droughts occur at regular intervals in many parts of the world. Some droughts are seasonal and take place every year during a dry period. People generally anticipate these droughts and the rainy seasons that usually follow. Researchers have also come to realize that some of the world's regions have **cyclical** *(SIK luh kuhl)* **droughts.** Such droughts occur at regular intervals, sometimes many years apart.

Monsoon climate

The **monsoon** is a seasonal wind that blows over the Indian Ocean and southern and southeastern Asia. It arrives from the southwest from June to September, bringing a great deal of rain. Then it blows

People desperate for water gather around a well in the Indian state of Gujarat after many wells, reservoirs, and ponds in the region ran dry during a drought in 2003.

from the northeast from December to March, creating generally dry conditions. If the dry season lasts longer than usual, drought often occurs. An unusually stormy wet season often brings floods. Such a pattern affected the state of Orissa in eastern India in 2001. Early in the year, drought conditions persisted over two-thirds of the state, affecting 11 million people and devastating 80 percent of the food crop. By July, Orissa was experiencing its worst flooding in 50 years, affecting nearly 10 million people.

The El Niño effect

Drought cycles are influenced by a climate effect in the Pacific Ocean known as **El Niño,** a term that means *boy child* in Spanish. El Niño, which refers to the Christ Child, got its name because it often begins around Christmastime. An El Niño event occurs about every 2 to 7 years and lasts for about 18 months. During an El Niño, an upper layer of warm water in the western Pacific flows eastward instead of in its normal westerly direction. El Niño causes increased rainfall along the west coast of North and South America and, at the other extreme, drought in Indonesia and Australia. During the El Niño of 1997-1998, Indonesia's dry season lasted for eight months instead of the usual three. The rice crop was so much smaller than expected that the country was forced to import more than 5.5 million tons (5 million metric tons) of rice. Forest fires burned out of control, damaging more than 24 million acres (10 million hectares) of land.

THE WATER GAP BETWEEN RICH AND POOR

Many water experts believe that a crisis exists not because there is a shortage of water in the world but because much water is wasted and does not reach people who need it. According to researchers at the 4th World Water Forum, which took place in Mexico City in March 2006, people living in developed nations use an average of 110 to 130 gallons (400 to 500 liters) of water per day. In developing countries, people use an average of 5 gallons (20 liters) per day. International representatives to the water forum recommended both encouraging people in developed nations to conserve water and helping governments in areas with water shortages to find ways to provide more water to their people.

Fire devours rain forest vegetation parched by an El Niño-related drought on the Indonesian island of Borneo in 1997.

ON THE GREAT PLAINS

The grasslands of the southern Great Plains are regularly subject to drought, during which grasses dry up and top soil is blown away.

The Great Plains region of North America is a vast, dry grassland. It stretches for 2,500 miles (4,000 kilometers) from northern Canada to Texas in the United States and for 400 miles (640 kilometers) east of the Rocky Mountains. A wide variety of natural grasses grow there. The region is also one of the world's major wheat-growing areas and produces such other crops as alfalfa, barley, oats, and rye. Cattle, goats, and sheep graze in the Great Plains. The area is regularly subject to droughts.

Studying cycles

Researchers have found that droughts have struck the Great Plains at regular intervals for thousands of years. By studying mud deposits at the bottom of a lake in North Dakota, they found that major droughts occurred at roughly 160-year intervals. The researchers examined tiny fragments of plants and charcoal, as well as seeds and pollen, to identify periods of high growth and periods when growth was poor because of drought. The results showed that droughts frequently led to grassland fires, which left the soil bare and caused dust storms, so that little grew for many years. As the rains returned, so did the grasses, starting the cycle all over again.

Dry farming

During the 1900's, droughts began to occur more frequently on the Great Plains, in cycles of about 20 to 23 years. Many scientists attributed this change to farming practices introduced by early settlers. The farmers brought with them plows that cut deeply into the soil. Later, mechanized tractors allowed them to farm not only more land, but also land that might have been considered unworkable in the past. Overgrazing added to the problem, and the land soon became **eroded.**

By the late 1930's, some farmers had learned a technique called *dry farming.* Using this method, farmers leave part of their land unplanted each year so that the soil stores moisture for the next year's crop. However, most Great Plains farmers in the 1930's owned small plots of land and needed every acre to grow crops to support their families. **Conservation** was a luxury few could afford, and the practice was not used enough to stop the widespread erosion of the soil.

Black sunspots are relatively cool patches surrounded by brown, warmer areas on the hot yellow surface of the sun in a close-up image taken through a solar telescope. Scientists suggest that droughts on Earth are more likely to occur during periods with less sunspot activity.

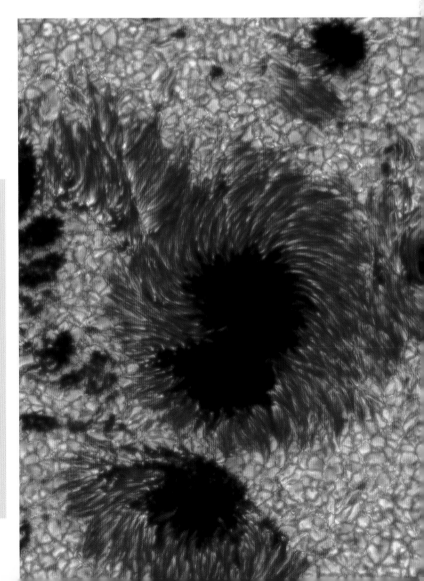

SUNSPOT LINK?

Scientists have found evidence that dry periods on Earth occur in cycles that correspond with cycles of magnetic activity on the sun. The sun is most active—and its magnetic field is strongest—every 11 years. At that time dark, cooler patches called **sunspots** form on its surface. Some scientists have suggested that droughts are more likely to occur during periods with less sunspot activity. Sunspot activity could explain the drought cycle on the Great Plains in the 1900's, which some experts believe followed a double sunspot cycle lasting 22 years.

WILDFIRES

Fire is one of the most devastating results of drought. When plants dry out because of lack of water, they act as **tinder** for the slightest spark. Once a blaze starts, it can spread rapidly through dry litter lying on a forest floor or across dried-out grassland.

Setting fires

When conditions are dry, forest managers often light fires deliberately in a specific area to burn off such materials as dry leaves and grass that could serve as fuel for more destructive fires. Such fires are called **prescribed fires.** They can be contained by clearing a strip of forestland, called a **firebreak,** to prevent the fire from spreading any farther.

In May 2000, a prescribed fire was set in a New Mexico forest after a long drought. But because of the dry conditions, the fire began to burn fiercely, sparking new fires beyond the firebreak. By the following morning, the fire had become a raging **wildfire**

The Cerro Grande fire burns out of control in May 2000 near Los Alamos, New Mexico, where about 18,000 residents had to leave their homes.

that was given the name Cerro Grande. Blown by strong winds across the town of Los Alamos, the blaze destroyed 235 homes and caused billions of dollars in damage. Cerro Grande was just one of thousands of forest fires—most of them occurring naturally—that raged across several parts of the United States in the spring and summer of 2000. Together, these fires burned more than 7 million acres (2.8 million hectares) of forest.

Part of the cycle

In forests that normally receive a reasonable amount of rainfall, dead wood, twigs, and leaves can build up on the ground for decades or centuries. This sets the stage for an intense fire when a drought occurs. Fires may strike such forests as rarely as once every 150 to 300 years, but these fires tend to be huge. However, once the fire is over, the ash from the burned grass and trees fertilizes the forest soil, helping healthy new plants—including trees—to grow. Some plants even rely on fire to reproduce. The cones of lodgepole pines, for example, release their seeds only when exposed to intense heat, such as during a fire.

Young pine trees grow quickly to restore a forest in Yellowstone National Park after severe wildfires in 1988 burned across more than 795,000 acres (321,000 hectares).

ASH WEDNESDAY FIRES

By early 1983, most of the Australian state of Victoria had experienced drought for at least 10 months. Rainfall over the summer (December to February in Australia) was up to 75 percent lower than in previous years. On February 16, more than 100 wildfires started. Some fires apparently started from sparks from electric power lines, set off by strong winds blowing the lines together. The same strong winds blew the fires across Victoria and South Australia, leaving a trail of devastation and killing 75 people. They came to be known as the Ash Wednesday fires, for the day on which they started. More than 1 million acres (400,000 hectares) of land burned in Victoria.

DEFORESTATION

During the 1990's and early 2000's, people worldwide cut down more trees and cleared more areas of forest than they planted. Before people began to clear the land for farms and cities, forests covered about 60 percent of Earth's land area. Today, forests occupy about 30 percent of the land. Such **deforestation** has many damaging effects on the **environment** and increases the risk of drought.

Creating drought

Trees help to create rainfall, and so the removal of trees has a direct impact on the amount of rainfall in a region. Areas of forest normally increase **humidity** in the atmosphere through **transpiration** *(TRAN spuh RAY shun)*—the process by which water **evaporates** from the leaves on trees. A birch tree may give off 70 gallons (265 liters) of water as vapor a day. The vapor rises, cools, and **condenses** into water, eventually falling back to Earth as rain. Transpiration may account for as much as half of the rainfall in some rain forests.

Rain clouds build up from the water vapor given off by rain forests in Central America. Cutting rain forests reduces rainfall, changing regional climate.

When a tree is cut down, much of its wood may be burned as fuel. Burning releases carbon dioxide into the atmosphere. Carbon dioxide is a **greenhouse gas** that traps heat in the atmosphere and contributes to **global warming.**

Problems in Pakistan

Pakistan has a dry **climate** with an average rainfall of only about 10 inches (25 centimeters) a year. It also has very little forest cover—less than 3 percent of its area—and a high rate of deforestation. From 1990 to 2005, Pakistan lost about 1.5 million acres (625,000 hectares) of forest, nearly one-fourth of its forest cover. The loss of trees is one of the most serious environmental issues affecting Pakistan today. During its short **monsoon** season, the rains are often so torrential that the water flows away over the surface of the hard, parched ground instead of soaking in and being taken up by tree roots.

DROUGHT EXPERIMENT

American researchers created a drought in the Amazon rain forest in the early 2000's so that they could monitor its effects. They hung 5,600 plastic panels above the forest floor over an area of 2.5 acres (1 hectare) so that most rainfall did not reach the ground. During the five-year experiment, many trees survived a lack of rainfall for a while. Some sent their roots as deep as 43 feet (13 meters) to find water. Others began taking in water through their leaves, a process scientists had never observed in trees before. Nevertheless, after two years, many trees began to die from lack of water. In addition, the gaps in the forest left by the dead trees allowed more light to reach the forest floor, making the ground even drier and increasing the risk of fire.

A villager wades through floodwater caused by severe monsoon rains in southern Pakistan, 2003.

A once-wide Amazonian tributary has become a meandering stream because of a severe drought that began in 2005.

The Amazon rain forest is the world's largest **tropical** rain forest. About two-thirds of it lies in Brazil. The remainder occupies parts of Bolivia, Peru, Ecuador, Colombia, and Venezuela. The Amazon rain forest receives an average annual rainfall of 50 to 175 inches (130 to 445 centimeters) and contains a wider variety of plant and animal life than any other place in the world. Tens of thousands of plant **species** live there. An area of the forest measuring 2.5 acres (1 hectare) may contain more than 280 species of trees. But the forest is being cleared at a rapid rate, and in 2005 and 2006, it suffered a severe drought.

Rain forest destruction

The leading cause of **deforestation** in the Brazilian Amazon is the clearing of land for cattle ranching, to produce beef. Such activity accounts for nearly two-thirds of the cleared land. An additional one-third of the land is cleared by small farmers who struggle to feed their families by growing crops on the forestland. The farmers usually clear the land by burning the rain forest, and the fires have frequently gotten out of control and destroyed large areas of forest.

Environmental disaster

The Amazon River, which flows through the rain forest, is fed with water from more than 200 **tributaries.** In 2005, the entire region suffered its worst drought in more than a century. Some of the Amazon's main tributaries—usually more than a mile (1.6 kilometers) wide—dried up completely. Others turned into mudflats, leaving boats stranded among millions of dead, rotting fish. The drought returned in 2006. Government officials said the drought was linked to record warm water temperatures in the Atlantic Ocean. But **environmentalists** believe that deforestation is also to blame.

SMOKE COVER

Scientists studying the Amazon reported in 2004 that smoke from burning fires in the rain forest can keep rain from falling. The smoke contains many more tiny solid particles called *aerosols* than are usually found in the atmosphere. An overabundance of aerosols prevents the formation of raindrops. The result is less rainfall, leading to an increased likelihood of drought. Their research confirmed the findings of an earlier study in Indonesia, which also showed that forest fires reduce rainfall. Such reports indicate that human activity can affect **climate** much more than people once believed.

Dead fish litter the dried banks of an Amazon tributary near Manaquiri, Brazil, in October 2005, the result of severe drought.

DESERTIFICATION

The world's deserts—generally defined as dry regions that get less than 10 inches (25 centimeters) of rain a year—cover about one-fifth of Earth's land area. They are unsuitable for growing crops or raising most kinds of livestock. When fertile soil in other areas **erodes** either because of drought or such practices as overgrazing, it becomes unproductive. This process through which fertile lands are destroyed or degraded is called **desertification** *(DEHZ uhr ti fi KAY shun).*

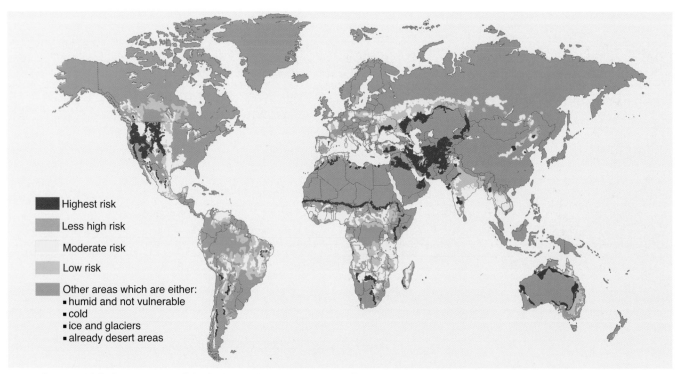

Highest risk

Less high risk

Moderate risk

Low risk

Other areas which are either:
- humid and not vulnerable
- cold
- ice and glaciers
- already desert areas

Source: U.S. Department of Agriculture, Natural Resources Conservation Service, Soil Survey Division.

Areas of the world at greatest risk from desertification.

A global problem

Desertification is a global problem. According to United Nations experts, about one-third of Earth's land surface is threatened by desertification. About 24 billion tons (22 billion metric tons) of fertile soil disappears every year, and the process directly affects more than 250 million people. The Sahel *(sah HEHL)* region of northern Africa, northwestern China in Asia, and the western United States in North America are all at very high risk of desertification.

Stopping the desert in its tracks

In some places, steps have been taken to prevent further desertification. For example, people have planted trees or shrubs at the edge of some desert areas—such as the Sahel—to act as windbreaks. The trees and shrubs reduce the strength of the wind at ground level and prevent sand from being blown onto crops. Wooden fences, called sand fences, are used in the Middle East and the United States to achieve the same effect. In China, the government began a project in 1978 to build a "green wall" of trees across the northern region of the Gobi Desert. According to the Chinese Environmental Protection Agency, this desert grew by 20,200 square miles (52,400 square kilometers) from 1994 to 1999. The 2,800-mile (4,480-kilometer) "wall," which is to be completed by 2050, is designed to keep the sands from spreading farther.

ITS OWN SPECIAL DAY

Even desertification has its own special day. The United Nations has set aside June 17 as the World Day to Combat Desertification. The day is part of a campaign by the international organization to call attention to the problem of desertification and to work on solutions. In 1994, world governments adopted the Convention to Combat Desertification, and it came into force in 1996. The 110 countries of the world affected by desertification have developed action programs through which they try to deal with desertification within their own borders and share their research findings with one another.

Workers in China check grasses that have been planted to stabilize sand dunes at the fringe of a desert.

IN THE SAHEL

The Sahel region spans the continent of Africa, on the southern borders of the Sahara.

The Sahel is a dry grassland in Africa. It lies south of the Sahara and stretches through large parts of Senegal, Mauritania, Mali, Burkina Faso, Niger, Nigeria, Chad, and Sudan. Some geographers also include the very dry regions of Eritrea, Ethiopia, Kenya, and Somalia as part of the Sahel. A number of serious droughts have struck this area, especially since 1968, causing the deaths of millions of people.

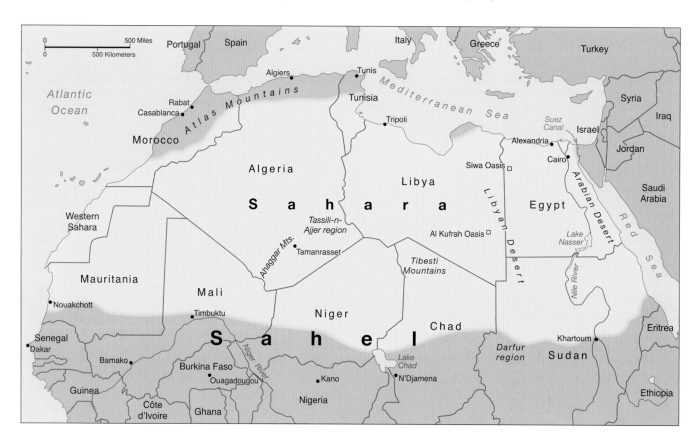

Shore of the Sahara

The term *Sahel* comes from an Arabic word meaning *shore* or *border*. This dry region got its name from the fact that it borders the Sahara, whose name also comes from an Arabic word that means *desert*. **Erosion** of the soil from overgrazing, as well as frequent droughts, have led to the **desertification** of large areas of the Sahel. As the land becomes desolate and unproductive, the sands of the Sahara move in, expanding the desert southward. In some places, sand dunes have buried entire villages. From about 1996 to 2006, 160,000 square miles (414,000 square kilometers) of previously usable land disappeared.

Years of drought

Researchers have found that droughts occur regularly in the Sahel, generally every 25 to 35 years. There were major droughts in 1910, 1940, 1970, and 1984. In addition, from the late 1950's to the late 1980's, rainfall decreased throughout the area. Herders had been accustomed to moving their livestock into the desert during the rainy season and returning to the Sahel during the dry season, which in many parts occurs from November to April. In 1968, there was no rainy season. Herds of cattle brought to drink from dwindling wells destroyed the vegetation around them, causing severe soil erosion. Crops failed, and as many as 250,000 people starved in the **famine** that followed.

CLIMATE REFUGEES

As drought continues in the Sahel, many people are losing their livelihoods and are being forced to leave their homelands. **Environmentalists** call these people **climate refugees,** because they believe that this long-term drought is a result of climate change caused by **global warming.** In the Mandera region of northern Kenya, seasonal herders are leaving their traditional lands because the lasting drought has killed so many of their cattle, camels, and goats. Those who do stay live in settlements beside rivers. But without their traditional ways of life, which they have followed for centuries, it is difficult for them to support themselves.

Women and children in central Mali travel many miles every day to fetch water to take back to their village.

FAMINE

Drought is one of the main causes of **famine**—a prolonged food shortage that causes widespread hunger and death. Throughout history, famine has affected certain regions of Africa, China, and India hardest because all of these regions have large areas near deserts, where the rainfall is light and variable. In the 1770's, severe drought in the Indian state of Bengal caused a famine that killed an estimated 10 million people. A century later, drought in China resulted in a famine that killed more than 9 million people.

A farmer on the Indonesian island of Java crosses a rice paddy that has dried up during a drought in 2003.

Crop failure

Drought that is followed by crop failure and famine is especially likely to occur in places where people can produce only enough food to feed their families. This way of life is known as **subsistence** (suhb SIHS tuhns) **farming.** In years during which crops grow well, subsistence farmers may produce more food than they need and can sell the surplus. But in drought years when crops fail, there is no food, and poor farmers cannot afford to buy produce that may be available at local markets. As famine takes hold, food supplies for people and animals begin to run out. Undernourished animals stop producing milk, and many are killed for food. In these circumstances, subsistence farmers are often forced to eat their seed. But when the rains finally return, there are no seeds to plant. With no crops and no livestock, people starve. The cycle of famine in developing countries is difficult to break without the help of food aid from other, richer countries.

Malnutrition and disease

People who do not eat enough food lose weight and grow weak. They become **malnourished.** During a famine, elderly people and young children are most at risk for malnutrition. Famines also increase the risk of **epidemics.** Large numbers of people may flee their homes during times of famine and live in refugee camps, where food aid may be available. But crowded and often **unsanitary** conditions in refugee camps can lead to outbreaks of diseases such as **cholera** *(KAHL uhr uh)* and **typhus** *(TY fuhs).* Such outbreaks are all the more deadly because malnourished people do not recover easily from disease.

A woman gives some water to her young child who is suffering from malnutrition as a result of severe drought and famine in Niger in 2005.

HUNGER FACTS

The United Nations World Food Program was established in 1962 to provide food aid to people in need worldwide. According to the organization,

- The world produces enough food for everyone. Yet 852 million people do not have enough to eat.
- Drought is the main cause of food shortages in poor countries.
- Six million children under age 5 die every year from malnutrition and hunger-related diseases.

CRISIS IN AFRICA

Drought has caused terrible **famines** in northeastern Africa throughout the centuries. In 1984 and 1985, such conditions—along with a civil war—struck northern Ethiopia, killing about 1 million people. Most Ethiopians are **subsistence farmers** or livestock herders who produce just enough food to feed their families. Their way of life makes them especially vulnerable to drought. The horrors of this famine prompted organizers to stage charity concerts in Philadelphia and London to help the people of Africa.

ROCKING FOR RELIEF

To raise money for the starving people of Ethiopia, Irish singer and songwriter Bob Geldof, together with Scottish singer and songwriter Midge Ure, wrote an original single called "Do They Know It's Christmas?" They formed a group of 38 British and Irish pop stars under the name Band Aid and recorded the song in November 1984. The recording eventually raised $10 million worldwide. In July 1985, Geldof and Ure organized simultaneous concerts in Philadelphia and London to raise money for Ethiopia. The Live Aid concerts, which were broadcast to an estimated 1.5 billion television viewers in some 100 countries, featured such performers as Joan Baez, David Bowie, Bob Dylan, Mick Jagger, Teddy Pendergrass, Led Zeppelin, U2, and the Who. The final total for funds collected as a result of the concerts was nearly $284 million.

A water truck arrives at a distribution point on March 16, 2006, in Dambas, Kenya, where thousands of people are facing starvation and thirst because of an extended period of drought.

Ethiopia 1984

In 1984, civil war in Ethiopia worsened a situation already made difficult by famine. Rebels opposed to the Ethiopian government controlled four drought-stricken provinces and prevented relief supplies from getting to the people who needed them. More than 6 million people faced starvation. On October 24, a reporter in Ethiopia for the British Broadcasting Corporation (BBC) described the situation as "a biblical famine, now, in the 20th century." Many people in Western countries were shocked by the photographs of **malnourished** Ethiopians that they saw on television night after night. People in Europe and North America donated money to provide food and medicine and to charter planes to help distribute relief supplies. But all these efforts could not prevent large numbers of deaths. By the end of 1984, as many as 900,000 people may have died in Ethiopia.

The government interferes

In 1985, Ethiopian officials prevented food supplies from being delivered to rebel-held areas and even diverted them to their own troops, who were fighting the rebels. The situation was so bad that an estimated 2,000 refugees a day fled the country for camps in neighboring Sudan. By then, the Western public had donated nearly $130 million.

People wait for food aid at a refugee camp in Ethiopia in 1991, when drought again struck the region.

AUSTRALIA'S EPIC DROUGHT

An Australian farmer inspects a dried-up reservoir on his land in 2002 during the start of one of the worst droughts Australia has ever experienced.

By 2007, many areas of Australia were experiencing their sixth year of drought—a drought that some scientists considered to be the worst to affect the continent in 1,000 years. In Queensland, Premier Peter Beattie announced in January that unless conditions changed, people in the state would be forced to drink recycled sewage water in 2008. In March 2007, camel experts warned that the country's 1 million *feral* (wild) camels were being driven mad by thirst. The animals were reported to have trampled fences, tanks, pipes, and Aboriginal sites in their frantic search for

water. In April, Australian Premier John Howard stated that the nation may be forced to cut **irrigation** to the Murray-Darling River basin. The basin is Australia's main agricultural region and produces about 40 percent of the nation's farm crops.

Farmers in New South Wales inspect their cattle, as the Australian drought continued into 2007.

A cycle of droughts

Some scientists believe that Australia may have a 50-year cycle of drought. The country experienced severe droughts in the 1850's, from 1895 to 1902, in the 1940's, and in the early 2000's. Other scientists see a connection between the drought that began in 2002 and the **El Niño** that ended in early 2007. During an El Niño, the western coast of South America is flooded with rain while the eastern coast of Australia becomes extremely dry. In 2006, Australian farmers harvested the smallest wheat crop in 12 years, and the barley harvest was about two-thirds the size of the previous year's. The Australian government offered special relief payments to farmers to help them support themselves during the drought.

DROUGHT BRINGS OUT DEADLY SNAKES

Australia is home to 10 of the most deadly snake **species** in the world. Usually, such snakes prefer to stay away from people. They live in the *bush* (remote countryside) and generally stay hidden. However, by 2007, the long-standing drought had dried up wide areas of bushland, and thousands of snakes moved into urban areas in search of moisture. Within the first few weeks of 2007, at least five city dwellers had been bitten by deadly snakes, and three of them had died from the poison. The victims lived in such large metropolitan areas as Sydney and Melbourne, and several of them were bitten as they weeded their gardens.

LIVING WITH DROUGHT

Some forecasters warn that the incidence of severe drought will increase during the 2000's and that nearly one-third of the world's land surface may be at risk of extreme drought by 2100. Experts found that during the 1990's, droughts were generally more widespread than earlier in the 1900's. Many researchers believe that **global warming** is to blame. Although no one knows what will happen in the future, many scientists believe that people in various parts of the world will have to learn to live with more frequent droughts.

Conserving soil

During the Dust Bowl disaster of the 1930's, the U.S. government established the Soil **Conservation** Service, now called the Natural Resources Conservation Service (NRCS). The goal of the agency was to teach farmers ways to slow **erosion** and to protect the soil. Experts in forestry, biology, and other sciences made soil surveys and developed conservation plans for individual farms. They encouraged—and helped finance—the planting of thousands of trees to act as windbreaks. They also introduced such methods as contour farming, strip cropping, and terracing. Contour farming

A farmer and a Conservation Service technician check an irrigation pipe in a corn field in Grant County, Washington.

required farmers to plow across slopes rather than up and down. The resulting ridges in the ground prevented water from flowing away down the slope and so helped to retain moisture in the soil. For strip cropping, farmers planted grass in strips between their crops. The grass held water and protected the soil. Farmers also built wide terraces on hillsides to hold rainwater and to prevent soil erosion. Finally, the experts urged small farmers to expand the variety of crops they grew beyond wheat and to consider using the land for the purpose to which it was best suited—grazing. Today, the NRCS continues to help farmers and land managers conserve their soil, water, and other natural resources.

Water conservation

In addition to conserving soil, one of the best ways to tackle the potential problems of drought is to conserve water. Farmers can practice dry-farming techniques, improve their **irrigation** methods, and select the crops that are most suitable for their soil and climate conditions. Some crops, such as sorghum, can survive with little moisture. City dwellers can do their share, too. People who live in cities are encouraged to install toilets that flush using less water, to take showers instead of baths, and to landscape their gardens with plants that are native to the area and require less water than plants that are accustomed to more humid conditions.

DROUGHT-RESISTANT BEAN

The guar, or cluster bean, is a drought-resistant plant of the pea family. It was first grown in India and was introduced into the United States in 1903. In Asia, guar beans are eaten as a vegetable. The crop is also grown for cattle feed and is plowed into fields to improve the soil. Guar can grow in high temperatures and with little moisture. When the soil is very dry, the plants stop growing, but they do not usually die. In the United States, gum from the beans is used to make paper and cloth. India, Pakistan, and the United States are the main producers of guar.

A farmer takes his sorghum crop to market in the East African country of Somalia, where droughts occur frequently.

SOIL EROSION EXPERIMENT

Plants help to protect soil from erosion by wind and water. This was a hard lesson learned by farmers in the Dust Bowl. When rains return after a drought, bare soil is easily washed away. You can do your own simple experiment to compare the effects of erosion on dry, bare ground and moist, planted soil.

Equipment
- 2 aluminum roasting pans
- soil
- grass seed
- 2 blocks of wood

1. Ask an adult to help you make a row of holes at one end of each pan.

2. Fill the pans with soil. Sprinkle grass seeds on one pan and rake them into the soil with a fork. Keep the soil moist. Leave the soil in the other pan bare and dry.

3. When the grass is an inch (several centimeters) high, put blocks under the pans so that they slope downward toward the ends with the holes.

4. Put a bowl beneath the pans to catch water. Then pour the same amount of water from the same height onto the higher end of the pans. Watch how much soil is washed away through the holes of each pan. You will see that the pan with grass growing in it loses less soil. The plants help to hold the soil in the pan.

agricultural drought A type of drought in which conditions in an area—such as precipitation and water level—fall below what the crops in the area need to grow.

atmospheric pressure The downward force caused by the weight of the air pressing on Earth's surface.

cholera A water-borne disease caused by bacteria.

climate The average weather in an area over a period of time.

climate refugees People who are forced to leave their homeland because a change in climate has deprived them of their traditional livelihood.

condense To change from a gas to a liquid as a result of cooling.

conservation The management, protection, and wise use of natural resources.

cyclical drought Drought that occurs at regular intervals, sometimes many years apart.

deforestation The clearing and removal of trees and forests.

desertification The process by which fertile land becomes unproductive.

El Niño A warming of the surface water of the sea off the western coast of South America and a related weather change that happens every two to seven years.

environment Everything that is outside an organism forms that organism's environment.

environmentalist A person who is concerned about and acts to protect the natural environment.

epidemic An outbreak of disease that attacks many people at the same time.

erosion Wearing away by the movement of water or wind.

evaporate To change from a liquid into vapor.

famine A prolonged food shortage that causes widespread hunger.

firebreak Land cleared of fuel to stop or slow the progress of a fire.

global warming The gradual warming of Earth's atmosphere over many years.

greenhouse gas A gas that traps heat in Earth's atmosphere, contributing to global warming.

groundwater Water held beneath Earth's surface.

headwaters The beginning and upper parts of a river.

heat wave A period of hotter-than-normal weather over at least several days.

humidity The amount of moisture (water vapor) in the air.

hurricane A tropical storm over the North Atlantic Ocean, the Caribbean Sea, the Gulf of Mexico, or the Northeast Pacific Ocean.

hydrological drought A type of drought in which surface and underground water supplies are low.

irrigate To water land by artificial means.

malnourished Weak and unhealthy because of a lack of adequate nutrition.

meteorological drought A type of drought during which there is less precipitation than usual in a particular area at a particular time.

meteorologist A scientist who studies and forecasts the weather.

monsoon A wind that reverses itself seasonally, especially the one that blows across the Indian Ocean and surrounding land areas.

precipitation Moisture that falls from clouds, such as rain, snow, or hail.

prescribed fire A fire that is set deliberately by forest managers to burn off materials that could feed a larger fire.

reservoir A place where water collects or is stored for use.

satellite An object that continuously orbits Earth or some other body in space. People use artificial satellites for such tasks as collecting data.

species A group of animals or plants that have certain permanent characteristics in common and are able to breed with one another.

subsistence farming A type of farming in which farmers are able to grow only enough food to feed their family.

sunspot A dark, cooler patch on the surface of the sun that appears when the sun is most active.

sunstroke Illness caused by exposure to too much of the sun's heat.

tinder Material that catches fire easily.

transpiration The process by which water evaporates from plants.

tributary A stream that flows into a larger stream or river.

tropics Regions of Earth that lie within about 1,600 miles (2,570 kilometers) north and south of the equator.

typhus Any one of a group of infectious diseases caused by rickettsias, a type of bacteria.

unsanitary Dirty and unhealthy.

water table The level of the groundwater below the surface of Earth.

weather system A particular set of weather conditions in Earth's atmosphere that affects a certain area or region for a period of time.

wildfire A fierce, destructive fire that spreads rapidly.

BOOKS

Drought, by Terry Jennings, Chrysalis, 2003.

Drought and Heat Wave Alert, by Paul Challen, Crabtree, 2004.

The Dust Bowl, by Ann Heinrichs, Compass Point Books, 2005.

Flooding and Drought, by Clive Gifford, Evans, 2005.

If It Rains: The Story of Droughts, by Dennis and Judith Fradin, National Geographic Children's Books, 2002.

Turbulent Planet: Heat Hazard—Droughts, by Claire Watts, Raintree, 2004.

WEB SITES

http://www.bom.gov.au/climate/drought/livedrought.shtml

http://drought.unl.edu/

http://www.drought.noaa.gov/

http://www.ens-newswire.com/ens/oct2005/2005-10-24-05.asp

http://www.worldwatercouncil.org/index.php?id=25

http://www.bbc.co.uk/weather/features/understanding/drought.shtml

http://www.wfp.org/aboutwfp/introduction/hunger_causes.asp?section=1&sub_section=1

INDEX